Presented to

_____

by

_____

on

_____

For Ava and Wrenna, Eleanor and Abigail.

❧

May you know how loved you are by God!
You're part of the ongoing story too...

GOD GAVE US THE BIBLE

All Scripture stories, quotations, and paraphrases are taken from the Holy Bible, New International Version®, NIV®. Copyright © 1973, 1978, 1984, 2011 by Biblica Inc.® Used by permission. All rights reserved worldwide.

Hardcover ISBN 978-0-7352-9190-4
eBook ISBN 978-0-7352-9191-1

Text copyright © 2019 by Lisa Tawn Bergren
Illustrations copyright © 2019 by David Hohn

Cover design by Mark D. Ford; cover illustration by David Hohn

Published in the United States by WaterBrook, an imprint of Random House, a division of Penguin Random House LLC.

WATERBROOK® and its deer colophon are registered trademarks of Penguin Random House LLC.

Library of Congress Cataloging-in-Publication Data
Names: Bergren, Lisa Tawn, author.
Title: God gave us the Bible : forty-five favorite stories for little ones / Lisa Tawn Bergren.
Description: First Edition. | Colorado Springs : WaterBrook, 2019.
Identifiers: LCCN 2018051009 | ISBN 9780735291904 (hardcover) | ISBN 9780735291911 (electronic)
Subjects: LCSH: Bible stories, English.
Classification: LCC BS551.3 .B473 2019 | DDC 220.95/05—dc23
LC record available at https://lccn.loc.gov/2018051009

Printed in China
2019

10 9 8 7 6 5 4 3 2

SPECIAL SALES
Most WaterBrook books are available at special quantity discounts when purchased in bulk by corporations, organizations, and special-interest groups. Custom imprinting or excerpting can also be done to fit special needs. For information, please email specialmarketscms@penguinrandomhouse.com or call 1-800-603-7051.

God Gave Us the Bible

45 Favorite Stories for Little Ones

by Lisa Tawn Bergren
art by David Hohn

WATERBROOK

Contents

It was a big day . . . the first day of summer.
And Little Cub was having a sleepover! After
playing outside, the children ate dinner on
the porch and then roasted marshmallows.

Later Mama Bear said, "Come into the house, kiddos.
I want to share a story with you. The best story ever!"

The kids came in and gathered around her.

"This is the story God gave us," she said, lifting her Bible. "It's really our story."

"Our story?" Little Pup said. "How can it be *our* story? Isn't it about a bunch of people who lived a long time ago?"

"God loved those people who lived a long time ago," she said. "Just as he loves us now. He wants us to know him better. That's why God gave us the Bible. Now, let's see," she said, turning to the first page. "It all starts with Genesis . . ."

"What does *Genesis* mean?" Little Cub asked. "It means the beginning," Mama said. "It's about the beginning of the world . . . and how God loved us from the start!"

The Creator Creates

Genesis 1

God is our Creator, the reason everything exists. He began with nothing; then he separated light from dark, and he made water and land. Next he made all kinds of animals and plants to fill them!

Imagine what it must've been like to see the first stars streaking across the night sky. To watch a garden springing to life, full of every flower you've ever smelled and every fruit you've ever tasted! Or to see the first whale slapping his gigantic tail in the sea!

Adam and Eve

Genesis 1–2

But God didn't stop there. Because he had a special plan . . .
to create children he could love! So he breathed life into
Adam and Eve. Adam got to name all the animals, and he

and Eve were given a very special place to live called the Garden of Eden.

Everything was good, *so* good. Adam and Eve spent their days hanging out with God and enjoying his creation. They didn't have to worry about a thing!

Leaving the Garden

Genesis 3

It was all good until a serpent said to Eve, "Did God *really* say not to eat any fruit in the garden?" Now, this was tricky because God didn't say such a thing!

Eve said, "We can eat fruit from any tree, but God told us not to eat from this one. If you eat from it, you will die."

"You won't die!" the serpent said. "You will be like God, knowing good and evil."

Be like God? Eve thought. *What could be wrong with that?*

So Eve plucked the nearest fruit and took a big bite of it. And when Adam came near, she talked him into doing the same.

At first it must've tasted as delicious as it looked. But as they ate, the fruit probably tasted sour—because they were committing sin, doing what God said not to do.

They knew they'd done wrong, so Adam and Eve got scared and hid from God, the one who loved them more than anyone could!

Because they had disobeyed him, God sent them out of the garden and into the world, where they would discover hard things. The world wasn't beautiful and peaceful like the garden. Yet even then, God was only beginning to write our story.

"That's sad," said Little Otter. "Why didn't God just put a fence around that one tree?"

"God wanted them to have a choice," Mama said. "Just like he gives us the choice today. He wants us to love him because we *choose* loving him, not because he *makes* us. But we often fail to do so— just like Adam and Eve."

"Like when I sneak an extra clam from the pot?" said Little Otter. "Even though my mama told me not to?"

"Exactly."

17

Noah's Ark

Genesis 6–9

After Adam and Eve left the garden, people gradually forgot God. They were mean to one another. No one believed in or talked to God. This made God very sad. By the time Noah lived, he was the only one who loved God with his whole heart!

So God told Noah to build a gigantic boat to hold a pair of every sort of animal you can name. From musk ox to monkeys, from weasels to wolves, from puffins to polar bears.

That ark must've seemed pretty crazy to Noah's neighbors, because the boat was *way* bigger than he'd ever need on a river!

But then the rain began . . . and it rained and rained. For forty days and nights, it rained!

Once the rain stopped, the ark still floated on top of all that water for months. Noah must've thought they were in the middle of an ocean. It was a happy day when he sent out a dove and she brought back an olive leaf! This meant a tree was growing somewhere and land *had* to be close.

After the ark finally scraped onto ground, God told Noah it was safe to bring out his family and the animals. He set a rainbow in the clouds as a sign—he would never send rain to flood the entire earth again. He'd found a way to begin anew with the people he loved and who loved him too.

"Hey, Mama, did Noah have a motor on that ark so he could steer?" Little Cub asked.

"No, he didn't. That's a good part of the story to think about. Noah had to trust that God would take that boat to the right place at the right time. And he did!"

God Chooses Abraham

Genesis 12–15

Many, many years passed, and lots of people lived in the world. But there was one special man named Abraham, who loved and followed God. God chose this man to further his plan to save the world forever.

He told Abraham that his children and grand-children would someday be as many as the stars in the sky! Abraham believed him even though he was old and he didn't have any children yet. And his wife was old too!

Because God had said, "Trust me. I will protect you and be your biggest, best reward."

Sarah Has a Baby

Genesis 21

Sarah thought Abraham was *cuh-razy* when he told her what God had said. She'd wanted a baby all her life, but she couldn't have one! And now she was way too old.

She was so surprised when she found out she was pregnant. Nine months later, she had little Isaac. And do you know what his name means? Laughter. Sarah and Abraham must've giggled in wonder every time they looked upon that boy. They were so happy God had given them a child. They loved him so much!

"Were they as old as Henrietta the Horned Owl?" asked Little Goose.

"Maybe," Mama said. "Can you imagine *her* having a baby owl now?"

"Nooooo!" cried the kids, laughing. Henrietta was so old she was losing feathers!

"Sometimes God does things that seem impossible to us," Mama said. "Like creating a whole nation starting with just one little boy—Isaac—born to old parents. We call those miracles!"

Joseph and His Cool Coat

Genesis 37

One of Abraham's grandchildren was named Jacob, who had twelve sons. And Jacob's favorite son was Joseph. His brothers were jealous that he was the favorite, and they got even more jealous when their father gave Joseph a beautiful coat!

Things got worse when Joseph started dreaming. First he dreamed that he and his brothers were all making stacks of wheat and that their stacks bowed down to his big stack of wheat.

Then he dreamed that the sun and the moon and eleven stars were bowing down to him. That made his father mad too, because they all wondered why young Joseph thought he was so cool.

Joseph Sold as a Slave

Genesis 37

Joseph's brothers were watching over flocks of sheep and goats in the hills. One day Joseph's father asked him to go see how they were doing.

When his brothers saw Joseph coming, they started grumbling. "Here comes that dreamer!"

"Let's kill him and throw him into a cistern," said one. (A cistern was a place they stored water in the ground.) "We can tell our father that Joseph was eaten by a lion!"

But as much as Joseph irritated him, Reuben, the biggest brother, didn't want to see him killed. "Let's just throw him in the cistern," he said, hoping he could come back and rescue him later.

So that's what they did.

But then some traders came by on their way to Egypt. "Hey! We don't get anything if we kill our brother," Judah said. "Let's sell him as a slave!"

The rest of them agreed. So they sold him, took his beautiful coat, dipped it in goat's blood, and brought it home to their father to make him think a wild animal killed their brother.

Jacob cried and cried when he thought his beloved Joseph had died.

"Wow," said Little Raccoon. "That was super mean of his brothers."

"Yes, it was," Mama said. "Sometimes jealousy can lead us to bad choices."

"Sometimes I get jealous of my brothers and sisters," he admitted.

"We all get jealous sometimes," Mama said. "God wants us to notice when we're feeling that way and choose to be loving and generous instead."

Joseph Imprisoned in Egypt

Genesis 39

Joseph was sold as a slave to a man named Potiphar, who worked for the king of Egypt. Joseph worked hard, and in time, Potiphar trusted him to run everything in his household.

All was going well until Joseph was blamed for something he didn't do, and he ended up in prison! Can you believe it? First a slave and then a prisoner! Poor Joseph must have thought his life had ended all over again.

Pharaoh's Dreams

Genesis 40–41

But God was with Joseph. Even in prison people knew he was special. He soon became the warden's favorite and helped others figure out what their dreams meant.

The king of Egypt, called Pharaoh, had a couple of crazy dreams, and he wanted help to make sense of them. But not one person he asked could do it.

Then a servant told Pharaoh about Joseph. Pharaoh sent for the young Hebrew. "I heard you can tell me what these dreams mean," he said.

"I can't," Joseph said. "But God can."

"Sometimes I have weird dreams," Little Moose said. "Do they all mean somethin'?"

"Probably not all of them," Mama said. "But some may! God was always speaking to Joseph, just like he does with us today. Through the Bible, through dreams, through thoughts that stick with us, and in other ways too."

Pharaoh asked Joseph what his two dreams meant.

"God is telling you what he's going to do," Joseph said. "There will be seven years with lots to eat followed by seven years when people might starve. We have to get ready!"

Deep down, Pharaoh knew this was God's own truth and freed Joseph from prison. But Pharaoh didn't stop there. He also made Joseph a prince in charge of the whole palace and ruler over all of Egypt!

For seven years Joseph went everywhere, collecting grain and storing it, preparing for the bad years to come.

Joseph's Brothers Go to Egypt

Genesis 42; 45

The bad years came, and everyone was starving. But Joseph's brothers heard there was still grain in Egypt, so they traveled there to buy some. As soon as Joseph saw them in the palace, he knew they were his brothers. But his brothers didn't recognize him. They'd sold him as a boy; now he looked like a man—an Egyptian man! Joseph didn't reveal who he was, but he sent them home with enough grain to feed their families.

The next year, they returned for more, and this time Joseph couldn't keep the secret any longer. "I am Joseph!" he cried to his brothers. "Is my father still living?"

Their father *was* still alive, but they could not answer him at first because they were scared to death! Here was the prince of Egypt, Pharaoh's right-hand man . . . the very brother they had sold into slavery. Would he kill them? Send them to prison?

"Don't be scared," Joseph said, hugging and kissing them. "God sent me here ahead of you to save you. Go home; then bring your families here, where you all will be safe."

"Hey," Little Pup said, "they bowed down to him just like he saw in his dreams!"

"And if he hadn't gone to Egypt, his family might've starved!" Little Otter said.

"Exactly," Mama said. "Sometimes it takes years to see it, but God is always working for our good. He even works through the hard things that happen in our lives."

Baby Moses Is Adopted

Exodus 1–2

The Hebrews moved to Egypt, and they had many, many children. They had *so* many children that Pharaoh was scared they'd take over his country, so he made them all slaves. Then Pharaoh told his men to kill every Hebrew baby boy.

One mother hid her baby boy for three months but knew she couldn't hide him much longer. So she got a basket, made it waterproof, and settled the baby in the reeds near the riverbank. Her daughter, Miriam, watched over the baby. She must have been so worried!

Do you know who found him? Pharaoh's very own daughter! She felt sorry for the crying baby, and she named him Moses.

Miriam told the princess that she could find a Hebrew woman to take care of the child until he was bigger. The princess agreed. Guess who Miriam went to get?

Moses's own mom!

"Moses's mother must've been so happy," Little Cub said.

"I bet she cried happy tears," Mama said. "His sister too."

"Why was Pharaoh so mean?"

"I think he was scared. Sometimes fear can make us do mean or evil things. But God had a plan in mind for Moses."

Moses Flees

Exodus 2

Moses got bigger, and he went to live in Pharaoh's palace. He was a prince of Egypt! But when he was all grown up, he saw how mean the Egyptians were to his own people and he killed one of them. This made Pharaoh very mad, so Moses ran away and became a shepherd.

For many years Moses lived in the mountains. He got married and took care of his sheep.

But for Egypt's slaves, life was getting worse and worse. God heard his people's cry and knew he must do something to save them.

The Burning Bush

Exodus 3

So one day God appeared to Moses, speaking to him from a
burning bush—a bush that stayed on fire but didn't burn up!
"Moses!" he called. "I am the God of your father, the God of
Abraham, the God of Isaac, and the God of Jacob."

Moses was so scared he hid his face.

"You're going to save my people and lead them to the Promised Land," God said.

Moses didn't think that would work—he wasn't much of a leader. But God said, "I will be with you."

"Moses had to go back and see Pharaoh? I bet that scared him too!" Little Cub said.

"Moses had to be brave," Mama said. "But he wasn't going alone. God promised to be with him."

"Kinda like how you or Papa come with me when I'm scared?"

"Exactly. And just like God was with Moses, he is with each of us, too, in good times and bad."

Moses Faces Pharaoh

Exodus 6–10

Things were about to get really hard for Pharaoh and the Egyptian people because Pharaoh didn't want to let his slaves go. Over and over, Moses told Pharaoh that God wanted his people free, but Pharaoh wouldn't listen. So God kept warning him—by sending terrible plagues.

First he turned the river Nile into blood.

Then he sent a plague of frogs. Millions of frogs hopping everywhere!

Gnats and flies came next—bazillions of them, covering the food, getting in their eyes and mouths. Yuck!

But Pharaoh still refused to let God's people go.

God sent more plagues.

Horses, donkeys, camels, sheep, goats, and cattle died.

People had sores all over their skin, from their heads to their toes.

Huge hailstones crashed down and smooshed crops.

Swarms of grasshoppers came and ate everything that was left.

Then it was dark—no sun or moon for three days!

Pharaoh begged Moses to make it stop and made promises that gave Moses hope. But every time, Pharaoh changed his mind about letting the Hebrews go.

Fleeing Egypt

Exodus 11–12; 14

Then came the very worst plague—the firstborn son of every Egyptian family, and the firstborn animal that every Egyptian owned, died. But the children and the animals of the Hebrews were spared.

Every Egyptian family was crying. Even Pharaoh, whose own son died. "Go!" he screamed at Moses. "Take your people and go!"

So the thousands and thousands of Hebrews gathered their things and began the long journey out of Egypt. But when they got to the Red Sea, they looked back and saw that Pharaoh's soldiers were chasing after them!

Parting of the Red Sea

Exodus 14

Moses called out, "Don't be scared! God is with us and will save us!" Then he stretched out his hand toward the sea, the water rose into walls, and a dry path appeared, leading to the other side!

The Hebrews ran through the channel, and the Egyptians came after them, but when his people made it to the other side, Moses stretched out his hand again. Just as God had told him, the water rushed back in and their enemies drowned.

"Whew," Little Moose said. "That Pharaoh was stubborn."

"Yes, he was," Mama said. "He refused to listen to God or to his servant Moses. We never want to be so stubborn that we can't hear God when he speaks to us. That's another reason God gave us the Bible," she said. "So we can learn from others."

Moses and the Ten Commandments

Exodus 16–17; 19–20

The Hebrews were a long way from the Promised Land and a long way from Egypt. They were hungry and thirsty and started to wonder whether they'd made a mistake, leaving their homes and food and water. Even after all they'd seen—being freed from slavery, watching the Red Sea part before them, and eating bread from heaven called manna—they were all very cranky. They were mad at Moses, God, and one another.

So God called Moses to a mountain. There was thunder and lightning! God wanted the people to know he was present. Then he gave Moses ten commandments. He wanted his people to love him as their only God. Not to steal or lie or kill or be jealous. To listen to their mamas and papas. He was telling the Hebrews how to stay close to him and find peace and joy together. Because he wanted that for his children, just as he does today.

David and Goliath

1 Samuel 17

Even when the Hebrews arrived in their new country, they still had enemies. One group called the Philistines was ready to attack. They had one of the biggest soldiers

ever seen—a giant named Goliath. He was over nine feet tall! He yelled at the Hebrews, daring them to send a man to fight him, but no one would.

Then David, a shepherd boy, went to visit his brothers on the battlefield. He asked, "Why are we letting him tease us? We're the army of God!"

He went to the king and said, "I've been taking care of my father's sheep, and I've fought off bears and lions. The Lord who saved me from those beasts will save me from this giant. Let *me* fight him."

"Wow!" Little Raccoon said. "That was brave!"

"It was," Mama Bear said. "But that's what trust in God does for us—it helps us be brave when we face problems that feel like giants!"

David went out to meet Goliath with nothing but his staff, his sling, and five stones. Goliath made fun of him, seeing he was only a boy. But David said, "You have a spear and sword, but because God is with me, I will win this fight!"

With that, he ran toward the giant, put a stone in his sling, and flung it at him. The rock hit Goliath right on the head, and he fell down dead!

Queen Esther

Esther 2–8

There was a powerful king in Persia named Xerxes, and he was looking for a new queen. His men looked everywhere for the most beautiful girls they could find, and after a long search, Esther was chosen from among them. Xerxes and Esther were married, and she became queen.

But Esther had a big, *big* secret. She was one of God's people, a Hebrew, also known as a Jew. And Xerxes's right-hand man *hated* the Jews. He hated them so much that he convinced the king to put them all to death!

The king agreed that on a coming day, every Jew in the empire would be killed.

Esther's cousin convinced her that she had to speak to the king about it. After all, she was the only Jew who would have a chance.

But Esther was scared. No one was allowed to go to the king unless they were invited. It was against the law, even for the queen!

Esther prayed and fasted (which means she didn't eat) and finally worked up the courage to go to the king. She must have been so relieved when he was happy to see her! The king asked her what he might give her . . . and she said, "Please save me and my people, the Jews."

And in the end, he did. Every Jew in the empire was saved!

"This story shows us that whoever we are and wherever we are, we can do God's good work," Mama said.

"Even me?" Little Cub asked.

"Every one of you," she said, looking around. "You are each a part of God's story too! Just like Esther and David!"

Shadrach, Meshach, and Abednego
Daniel 3

One day the king of Babylon built a huge statue, covered it with gold, and said everyone had to bow down and worship it. But Shadrach, Meshach, and Abednego said no, because they were Jews. They knew God wanted them to worship only *him*. It was one of the Ten Commandments!

This made the king very angry. He said, "Do as I say, or you'll be thrown into a hot furnace!"

They said, "Sorry, King, but we can't do it. God can save us from your fire. But even if he doesn't, we will not bow down to your fake god."

That made the king even more mad! He had his men fuel the fire until it was seven times hotter than normal and demanded that Shadrach, Meshach, and Abednego be thrown in.

But then the king saw the three of them walking around in that furnace, unharmed, and an angel was with them! "Come out!" he cried. And when they did, he saw that their clothes hadn't been touched by the fire. Not even their hair was burned!

"I just wanna worship God too," Little Owl said. "But I don't know if I would've been brave enough to stand up to the king."

"That'd be really hard, huh?" Mama said. "But I think what God wants us to see in *this* story is that we're called to be faithful, no matter what fires we face. And if we look to him when we're scared, he can help us be brave."

Daniel in the Lions' Den

Daniel 6

Another man who lived in Babylon was Daniel, one of King Darius's most important men. He was so good at his job that the king wanted to put him in charge of the whole empire. This made other men jealous, so they tried to figure out a way to get rid of him. One thing made Daniel stand out: he prayed to God three times a day.

So the men convinced the king to create a new law. The rule said that any person who prayed to anyone but King Darius himself would be thrown into a lions' den!

Sure enough, Daniel was caught praying, and the king was super sad because he was trapped by his own law—he had no choice but to throw Daniel in with a pack of hungry lions. All night, the king sat in his room, wondering what had happened to his favorite helper.

When he went the next morning to see, he found out Daniel was fine! "God shut the mouths of the lions!" Daniel cried.

"Everyone in my kingdom will pray to God just like Daniel does," King Darius said, "because his God rescued him from the lions!"

"So many of the stories in the Bible tell us about God rescuing his people," Mama said. "No matter how far they were from home, God was with them."

"How come he doesn't save everyone?" Little Cub asked. "You know . . . How come people die of sickness?"

"Or in an accident?" said Little Pup.

"Or from just getting really old?" said Little Moose.

"I don't know why God doesn't always save us here on earth," Mama said. "Sometimes we're not healed or rescued until we get to heaven. Remember when we talked about the Garden of Eden?"

"Like when Eve ate that fruit?" Little Pup said.

"Yes," Mama said. "That's when people started listening

to the Evil One and not to God. When they forgot God and made bad choices."

"Really bad choices," Little Cub said.

"Just like we do sometimes," Mama said. "But even when it all went wrong, God began to plan a way to save us. To make sure that we could live with him forever in heaven."

"How'd he do *that?*" Little Cub asked.

"Well, let's find out," Mama said, turning back to the Bible.

Mary's Miraculous News

Luke 1

God was about to change the world. You'd think he'd send an earthquake or an army! But instead he sent an angel to a young girl named Mary.

She was really scared when the angel appeared before her. "Don't be afraid," he said. "God loves you very much. You're going to have a baby, and you will name him Jesus."

"But I'm not even married yet!" she said. (Mary was engaged to a man named Joseph.)

"God is powerful and will make it happen. Your baby will be the Son of God. Even your cousin Elizabeth is having a baby in her old age. Because nothing is impossible with God."

"I am God's servant," Mary said.
"May it be as you've said."

Mary and Elizabeth

Luke 1

Mary was so excited she packed up her things and went to see Elizabeth, who lived in the country. As soon as she called out to her, the baby in Elizabeth's belly did a *somersault*!

Elizabeth laughed and stared at Mary, amazed. "You've been blessed, Mary! Blessed is the baby you carry! Even my own baby already knows him!"

Jesus Is Born!

Luke 2

When Mary was super pregnant, she and Joseph had to go to Bethlehem, and try as he might, Joseph couldn't find a place for them to stay. The city was very, very crowded.

One innkeeper said that they could stay in his stable. The Son of God wasn't going to be born in a palace or a mansion or a hospital. He was about to be born where animals slept!

"In a *barn?*" Little Cub asked.

"Well, yes. Their version of one back then," Mama said.

"But he was the Son of God!"

"Yes, but people didn't know that yet. Though they were about to . . ."

The night Jesus was born, shepherds were watching over their sheep. An angel came to them, saying, "I have good news for you! A Savior has been born!"

Then a bunch of other angels appeared around the first, all shouting and so, so happy! It had to be the most incredible celebration *ever*. "Glory to God!" they sang. "Peace on earth!"

"Let's go find this baby!" said a shepherd. And after they found him, they told everyone they met what had happened.

The Wise Men Find Jesus

Matthew 2

Some wise men came from the East because they knew a king had been born. They went to King Herod in Judea. "Where can we find the new king? We saw his star and came to worship him."

"Oh," said Herod. "I don't know. But when you find him, let me know so I can worship him too."

The star led them to Jesus, and they gave him gifts. They gave him gold, frankincense, and myrrh—gifts fit for a king!

After they left, an angel came to Joseph and said, "Quick! You need to take your family and run away because Herod will want to kill Jesus. I'll tell you when it's safe to come home."

Jesus Gets "Lost"

Luke 2

After Herod died, Mary and Joseph headed home, but they avoided the area where the new king ruled, moving to Nazareth instead. Joseph was a carpenter, and Mary looked after their family. Every year, they traveled to Jerusalem for the Feast of the Passover, a special holiday to help them remember how God saved his people in Egypt.

All the Jews did this, so there were a ton of people on the road. When Jesus was twelve, Mary and Joseph were partway home when they realized that he wasn't with them! They thought he was lost!

But when they got back to Jerusalem, they found Jesus listening to the Jewish teachers in the temple and asking them questions. Everyone around him was amazed at how much he understood, even as a kid.

"Jesus, we've been looking for you!" Mary cried. "We've been so worried!"

But Jesus explained, "Didn't you know I'd be in my Father's house?"

"What did he mean?" Little Pup asked. "That's not his house."

"Remember, Jesus is God's Son. So to him, God's holy temple—the Jewish version of a church—was as close to 'home' as he could get."

"Did he stay there forever, then?"

"Oh no. This story reminds us that he was Mary and Joseph's son too. So he went home with them to keep growing up. That's what made Jesus so unique—he was God's Son, but he was fully human too."

John the Baptist

Matthew 3

Remember the baby who did a somersault in his mama's womb when the pregnant Mary got close to him? Even before John was born, he knew Jesus was the Savior and his job was to get people ready to recognize God's Son too.

He went out to the desert and told people they must stop sinning because the kingdom of God had arrived. And then he baptized them in the river. "I baptize you with water, but there is one coming who will baptize you with the Holy Spirit!"

John was talking about Jesus, of course. And one day Jesus came to the Jordan River to be baptized.

John couldn't believe it! "Lord, it's you who should baptize *me*!"

But Jesus said, "Please do as I ask. This is how it's supposed to go." So John did.

When Jesus came up out of the water, God spoke from heaven. "This is my Son. I am so happy with him!"

"Why did God say that, Mama?"

"He wanted everyone to know how proud he was of his Son. God is proud of us too. He wants us to be washed by the water and become part of his own family. That's what Jesus shows us in this story."

"I love it when you say you're proud of me."

"I know, Little Cub," Mama said, squeezing her tight. "Imagine how Jesus felt!"

Jesus Calls the Disciples

Luke 5

Now Jesus was set to go. He knew what he needed to do—tell people the good news that the kingdom of God had arrived—but he wanted others to help him.

One day he was preaching beside the Sea of Galilee and a big crowd had gathered. Two brothers named Peter and Andrew stood beside their boats. It had been a *long* night, and they had caught very few fish.

"Go back out and put your nets in the water!" Jesus said to them.

Now, Peter didn't really want to. He was *so* tired. But there was something about Jesus that made Peter want to do what he said. And as soon as he did it, they caught so many fish it almost sank the boat! It was then Peter knew that Jesus was not just another regular person.

"Come and follow me," Jesus said. "And you can catch people instead of fish!"

Just like that, Jesus had his first two disciples. Ten others soon followed.

"What does *disciple* mean?" asked Little Pup.

"It means student or follower," Mama said. "Just like we're Jesus's disciples today! Back then, these were the very first people to truly listen to Jesus and watch what he was doing so they could be like him."

The Lord's Prayer

Matthew 6

The disciples and all the people around them had never met anyone like Jesus. It was like he knew God personally . . . because he did! Jesus showed them how to love and be kind and forgive others. And he taught them how to pray.

"Keep it simple," Jesus said. "Your Father in heaven already knows what you need before you ask him. But here is what you can say: 'Papa, you are amazing. Help us get what we need today—enough food and a roof over our heads. Forgive us for the ways we fail you, just as we forgive those who fail us. Rescue us from evil things and evil ways. Amen.'"

"Jesus taught them to call God Papa?" Little Cub asked.

"Yes, in his language it was *Abba*. Jesus used the same word when he prayed. He wanted to show us that God is as close as anyone who takes care of us and loves us."

Jesus Heals the Sick

Matthew 8–9

Jesus got more and more famous, and the crowds that followed him got bigger. He healed people—of fevers, skin diseases, blindness, and more!

Some men, having heard that Jesus was healing people, brought their paralyzed friend to him on a mat. He couldn't walk at all. "Be encouraged, son," Jesus said to him. "You are forgiven."

This made the religious leaders mad. *Only God can forgive someone!* they thought. *Who does this guy think he is?*

"Which is easier?" Jesus said to them. "Forgiving him? Or telling him to walk? I can do both." Then Jesus turned to the man and said, "Get up, take your mat, and go home." And the man did just that!

103

The Greatest Commandment

Matthew 22

One day a jealous leader tried to trap Jesus, asking, "Teacher, which is the greatest commandment in the Law?" (The Jews were no longer living by just ten commandments. There were hundreds of different rules!)

Jesus said, "Love God with everything in you. And love everyone around you like you love yourself." Well, that was a new idea! Those two rules would now top all the other rules. The leaders were speechless.

The Lost Sheep

Luke 15

The religious leaders kept following Jesus around. They couldn't figure him out. Jesus seemed to know God and the Scriptures better than they did, but he didn't act religious. They grumbled over the fact that Jesus hung out in the wrong part of town and ate with people they didn't like. They would never be caught hanging out with *sinners*.

Then Jesus told them this parable: "If you had a hundred sheep and one got lost, wouldn't you go after him? And when you found him, wouldn't you bring him home, happy that he was found?" Then Jesus looked at the leaders and said, "That's how God acts in heaven!"

"What's a parable?" Little Moose asked.

"It's a kind of story that Jesus used to help his followers understand truth," Mama said. "And it helps us understand God better too."

"So . . . am I the lost sheep in this parable or one of the others who didn't get lost?" Little Cub asked.

Mama gave that some thought. "At one point or another, most of us lose our way, Little Cub. And we become the

sheep that the shepherd leaves all the others to find. Just like I'd leave everyone to go find you if you were ever lost!" she said.

"Did he tell other parables?" Little Pup asked.

"Oh yes," Mama said. "He told of a lost coin and even a lost son! Let's read that story next."

The Prodigal Son
Luke 15

There was once a young man who went to his father and asked for his share of the family's money—something that usually happened only after a father died. This must've made his papa very sad, but the father did as his son asked and gave him the money.

The son left home, and he did things that he knew were wrong. After a while, his money was all gone. And then a famine came and everyone was *very* hungry.

The young man was so desperate he took a job feeding pigs. He even thought about eating the slop he was feeding them! *What am I doing?* he thought. *I should go back to my father's house. Even the people who work for him eat better than this! I should go see if he'll give me a job working for him.*

All the way home, he worried about how things would work out. *Papa's going to be so disappointed in me,* he probably thought.

But when his father saw him walking down the road, he did something the son never expected—his papa *ran* to him and hugged and kissed him! Then he called for new clothes and new shoes for his son . . . and he arranged a big party. "My son was lost," he said, "but now he's found!"

"So we're sometimes like the son, just like we're sometimes like the lost sheep?" Little Cub asked.

"Yes. Jesus wanted to show us that no matter how far we run from God— no matter what we do, no matter how ashamed we feel about the bad things we've done—God will run to meet us when we return to him."

Jesus and the Little Kids

Luke 18

Jesus had a special place in his heart for children. Everywhere he went, mothers and fathers brought their babies and kids to him so he could bless them. After a while, the disciples got tired of it and tried to tell them to go away.

But Jesus said, "Don't chase away the kids! The kingdom of God belongs to people like them! To enter the kingdom of God, you need to be like a little child."

"What does he mean, 'like a little child'?" Little Pup asked.

"Well, what are kids like? Most are curious, open, and loving, right? Full of faith and joy, like you," she said. "Kids trust that things will work out. It's harder to be like that when you're a grown-up. Jesus's reminder is a good one for us adults."

Jesus Calms the Storm

Mark 4

After a long day of teaching, Jesus said to his disciples, "Let's go to the other side of the lake." He was so tired he fell asleep in the back of the boat. Even when a storm came up, he kept on sleeping!

The waves got bigger and bigger and *bigger*. The disciples were really scared because some of the waves were coming into the boat! "Teacher," they said to him, "don't you care if we drown?"

Jesus got up and yelled, "Hey, WIND! Be quiet! Hey, WAVES! Be still!"

And the wind and the waves stopped. The disciples looked at him in amazement, then back out to the lake.

"Why were you so scared?" Jesus said. "Don't you believe yet?"

"Who is this?" the disciples asked one another. "Even the wind and the waves obey him!"

"So those guys had seen Jesus heal *all* those people, and they *still* didn't get it?" Little Cub asked.

"It's surprising, huh? Sometimes we don't get it either. When we face hard times—our own storms— we forget that God is with us. We need to remember that Jesus can see us through anything."

The Loaves and Fish

Mark 6; John 6

No matter where Jesus went, people raced to meet him. One time he even set sail in a boat to get some time alone. But when he arrived on the far shore, they found him again. By this time, *thousands* of people were following Jesus.

After Jesus taught all day, his disciples said he should send the people away to get something to eat.

"You give them something to eat," Jesus said.

"That'd be impossible!" they said. "It would take more than six months of working to feed them all!"

"How much food do you have?" Jesus asked.

"A little boy gave us five loaves of bread and two fish," they said.

Jesus told everyone to go sit in groups. Then he took the bread, looked toward heaven, and gave thanks. He sent the disciples out to feed them all, and somehow there was more than enough to feed every single person!

"Whoa," Little Otter said. "*Everyone* there got enough to eat?"

"God can do amazing things and knows what we need," Mama said, as Little Otter's tummy rumbled. "Even helping fill our hungry bellies!"

123

Lazarus Raised from the Dead

John 11

Jesus was out in the country when he got sad news. His friend Lazarus was very sick. Lazarus's sisters, Mary and Martha, wanted Jesus to come see him.

Several days later, Jesus arrived, but Lazarus had already died. Lots of people had gathered with the family to grieve with them. Martha said to Jesus, "If you'd been here, Lord, Lazarus wouldn't have died!"

"Your brother will rise again," he said.

125

"I am the resurrection and the life," Jesus said. "If you believe in me, you'll live—even when you die! Do you believe in me?"

"Yes, Lord," Martha said. "I believe that you're the Son of God."

Then Mary came out of the house, crying hard.

"Where have you put Lazarus?" Jesus asked.

"Over here," the sisters said and led him to a tomb. And there Jesus cried with them.

"Couldn't this man who heals the blind have come sooner to heal his friend?" whispered some people.

"Take away the stone," Jesus said.

"But it will be so stinky!" Martha said. "Lazarus has been dead four days!"

"Didn't I ask if you believed?" Jesus said. So the stone was moved away. Jesus looked up to the sky and said, "Father, thank you for hearing me." He turned to the tomb and called, "Lazarus, come out!"

Then his friend—once dead, now alive—came out, still wrapped in his graveclothes!

"Did he look like a mummy?" Little Moose said.

"Probably," Mama said. "In those days, when people died, they put special oil on them, wrapped them in cloth, and then buried them in tombs dug from the rock."

Mama got very quiet then. "This was a big moment for Jesus and the disciples. It's a big part of the story for us too. Some really bad things happened to Jesus after this. And some good things too. But I think he was trying to make sure all his disciples—including us—really understood. What did he say to Martha before he raised Lazarus?"

"He said he was the resurrection and the life!" Little Cub said.

"That's right."

"What does *resurrection* mean?" Little Goose asked.

"It means life, even after death. Remember that, sweet children. Now, to bed with all of you!"

During breakfast the next morning, Mama picked up her Bible again. "Do you want to hear more of the story?"

"Yeah!" cried the kids.

Palm Sunday

Matthew 21

The disciples and Jesus went to Jerusalem, with Jesus riding on a donkey. The people were going wild because news had spread of all that Jesus had done. They put their coats and palm branches on the road in front of him, treating him like a king and cheering for him!

Jesus went to the temple and healed more blind people and those who couldn't walk. Even the children were running around, shouting in their excitement, which made the religious leaders mad again.

The Last Supper

Matthew 26

But Jesus knew that all this celebration wasn't going to last long. "The Passover is two days away—and I will be handed over to be killed," he warned his disciples.

They didn't want to believe it.

Later, when they were celebrating the Passover Feast, Jesus picked up some bread, gave thanks, and broke it, saying, "Take and eat; this is my body."

Then he picked up a cup of wine, gave thanks again, and passed it to them, saying, "Drink this, all of you. This is my blood. Do this to remember me."

All the kids looked at her in alarm. "Why would they kill him?" asked Little Moose. "I mean, he only did good things! Healed people and stuff!"

"I know. It's hard for us to imagine. But God knew it was the only way. To sacrifice his own Son to cover our sins forever."

Jesus Dies

Matthew 27; John 19

Jesus was captured and taken to the man in charge of Jerusalem, Pontius Pilate. "Are you the king of the Jews?" Pilate asked.

"You have said so," Jesus said.

Every year, as the Passover Feast began, Pilate released a prisoner. Pilate asked the Jews which prisoner he should let go.

The religious leaders talked the crowd into calling for a different prisoner to be freed, not Jesus.

"What should I do with Jesus, then?" Pilate shouted.

"Kill him!" they said.

Then they made Jesus carry a cross up a hill. And he was hung on it and left to die.

His mother and his followers gathered at the foot of the cross, crying and crying.

The sky became very dark. And when Jesus took his last breath, there was an earthquake. It was like all of God's creation was crying with them.

"He *died?*" Little Cub asked.

"He did," Mama whispered, and a tear slipped down her cheek.

"Why?" demanded the rest of the kids.

"For you. For me. You'll see . . ."

Pilate gave Jesus's friend permission to take his body down and bury him in a tomb. The friend wrapped the body in cloth and prepared Jesus for burial. Then he put him in the tomb and rolled a rock in front of it to seal it.

The religious leaders remembered that Jesus said he would be resurrected on the third day, so they talked Pilate into having guards watch the tomb day and night so the disciples wouldn't steal his body.

Two days passed. And on the third . . .

The Resurrection

Matthew 28

Mary and Mary Magdalene were at the tomb when a big earthquake made the ground rock and roll beneath their feet!

An angel came down from heaven. The Roman guards were scared to death. The angel rolled away the rock in front

of the tomb. He looked at the women. "Don't be afraid. I know you're looking for Jesus. He isn't here; he is risen! Take a look."

They did as he asked, and he was right. Jesus's body was gone!

"Go and tell his disciples!" the angel said. "He is risen and you will see him again."

"Wait a minute!" Little Cub cried. "He came back to life?"

"Yes," Mama said with a smile. "He died for us, making a path to be with God. And he came back to show us what resurrection looks like, if we believe in him. That's what he meant when he said we'd live forever. When our earthly bodies die, we'll be with him and God in heaven with new bodies."

"What if I like this one?" Little Skunk said.

"Yeah!" Little Pup said. "What if we like this one?"

"Then you'll like your new body even *better*," Mama said. "And in heaven there will be no sickness or sadness. It will be like Adam and Eve experienced in the garden, at the very beginning of the Bible."

"So that was it?" Little Cub asked. "The disciples never saw Jesus again until heaven?"

"Oh no," Mama said. "Jesus appeared to them again on earth, proving he was very much alive. Let's read a bit more . . ."

Jesus Appears to the Disciples

Luke 24; Acts 1

The women came and told the men about the empty tomb, but they did not believe it. So Jesus showed himself to them. He walked with two of them on the road to Emmaus!

The men were so excited they ran back to Jerusalem to tell the others, and then Jesus appeared to *all* of them there. At first, everyone was scared because they thought he was a ghost!

But Jesus showed them he wasn't. "Touch me," he said. "I'm real—so real I'm hungry. Do you have anything here to eat?"

"That'd be cool if Jesus showed up right now!" Little Cub said.

"Yeah! Right here on the porch!" Little Pup said.

Mama smiled. "That would be cool. And he just might! That's part of the story!"

Jesus spent the next forty days teaching his followers. He explained that what God's prophets promised about a Messiah had been fulfilled in his birth, death, and resurrection. At last, the disciples really understood that Jesus was the Savior the world had been waiting for!

Jesus taught them more about the kingdom of God before he left for heaven. "The Holy Spirit is going to come and give you power," Jesus said. "And you'll tell everyone about me here and in the next town . . . and in all the world!"

Paul Sees the Light

Acts 9

Now, many people did not like the disciples or the new followers who believed in Jesus. One was named Paul. He wanted to track down Jesus's followers and put them in prison!

So Jesus appeared to him in a great flash of light. It was so bright Paul fell to the ground. "Who are you, Lord?" he asked.

"It's me, Jesus," he said. "When you're mean to my people, you're mean to me." Then he struck Paul blind! "Now go into the city and wait," he said.

In Damascus a man named Ananias came to Paul. "Brother," he said, putting his hands on him, "Jesus sent me here to heal you. You will be filled with the Holy Spirit." Right away, Paul could see! And he knew then that Jesus was real.

So Paul went from hunting Jesus followers to hanging out with them and then doing as they did—telling others about Jesus. And in them people saw such joy and peace, they wanted to become Jesus followers too.

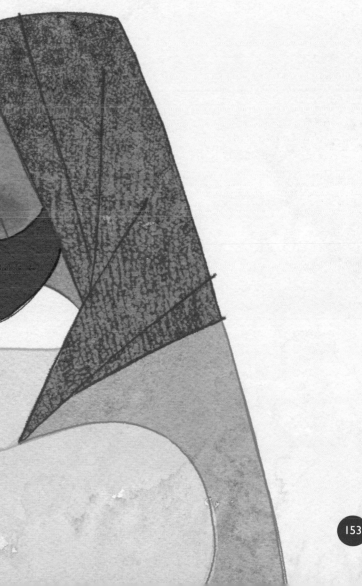

Paul Spreads the Good News

Acts 13–28

Paul went super far, telling everyone he could about Jesus. He was so sure that Jesus was the Savior, nothing could stop him from sharing what he knew! In his travels he suffered shipwrecks, time in jail, beatings, and hunger. But through it all, he remained faithful. Because of Paul, many people came to believe in Jesus.

And the generation of believers after him continued to tell the story . . . as did the generation of believers after *them* . . . and the next . . .

"And the next," Mama said. "Until it was my turn to tell the story to you kids. The story of God's love. Of Jesus's death and resurrection! Of him sending us the Holy Spirit. Of us someday living forever with Jesus in heaven. Now it's your turn, kiddos. Because God gave us this story," she said, lifting up her Bible, "not as a pretend story. But as the truest story of all."

"I know the truth," Little Cub said.

"Me too," said the other kids.

They were all silent for a second. Then Little Moose asked, "What's the Holy Spirit?"

"The Holy Spirit is God living in our hearts. He helps us know what's right and wrong. He comforts us when we're sad. And encourages us to be like Jesus. Do you want to be like Jesus?"

"Yes!" shouted the kids.

"That's how the story lives on," Mama said. "Through you. Through me. That's how it becomes *our* story."

"So . . . God really gave us a *never-ending* story," Little Cub said that night.

"That's right," Mama said. "Isn't that the best kind? Someday we'll see Jesus face to face and a whole new part of our story will begin!"

"I'm glad he gave us the Bible, Mama. I'm glad he loves us that much."

"Me too, Little Cub," she said, kissing her. "Me too."

Lisa Tawn Bergren is the best-selling author of nearly sixty books. Her beloved God Gave Us children's series has introduced children all over the world to God's unconditional love. Lisa and her husband, Tim, reside in Colorado.

David Hohn is an award-winning illustrator whose engaging art has graced many popular children's books. He graduated with honors from the Maryland Institute College of Art and has an MFA in Illustration from the University of Hartford. David lives in Portland, Oregon, with his family.